A FOUNDATION OF FAITH

BUILDING DEEPER FAITH

wesleyan
PUBLISHING HOUSE
wphstore.com

Copyright © 2015 by Wesleyan Publishing House
Published by Wesleyan Publishing House
Indianapolis, Indiana 46250
Printed in the United States of America
ISBN: 978-0-89827-284-0
ISBN (e-book): 978-0-89827-285-7

All Scripture quotations, unless otherwise indicated, are taken from the Holy Bible, New International Version®, NIV®. Copyright ©1973, 1978, 1984, 2011 by Biblica, Inc. Used by permission of Zondervan. All rights reserved worldwide. www.zondervan.com. The "NIV" and "New International Version" are trademarks registered in the United States Patent and Trademark Office by Biblica, Inc.

Scripture quotations marked (KJV) are taken from the HOLY BIBLE, KING JAMES VERSION.

Scripture quotations marked (NASB) are taken from the *New American Standard Bible*®, Copyright © 1960, 1962, 1963, 1968, 1971, 1972, 1973, 1975, 1977, 1995 by The Lockman Foundation. Used by permission.

Scripture quotations marked (ESV) are from The Holy Bible, English Standard Version® (ESV®), copyright © 2001 by Crossway, a publishing ministry of Good News Publishers. Used by permission. All rights reserved.

Portions of this book have been revised from these previously published books from Wesleyan Publishing House: *Knowing Christ* and *Growing in Christ*.

All rights reserved. No part of this publication may be reproduced, stored in a retrieval system, or transmitted in any form or by any means—electronic, mechanical, photocopy, recording, or any other—except for brief quotations in printed reviews, without the prior written permission of the publisher.

CONTENTS

For a free group leader's guide,
visit www.wphresources.com/building.

INTRODUCTION

Welcome to an exciting journey into deeper discipleship!

This book is part of the Building Deeper Faith series, offering believers at various levels a great opportunity for deeper spiritual growth. The entire series has been developed to help you grow as a disciple of Jesus Christ. By participating in this study with others (ideally in a group), you can discover and experience how God will shape your life according to his Word, especially by using spiritual disciplines such as Bible study, prayer, Scripture memorization, and journal writing.

THE GOAL: DISCIPLESHIP

Discipleship is the life-long process of spiritual development for those who commit their lives to following Jesus. It is far more about what it means to know and follow the person of Jesus Christ than merely gaining knowledge about him. So throughout this series, the strategy for making disciples will be measured in terms of how to build in relation to others — in relation to God, to his people, and to neighbors. This time-tested strategy is built upon four core biblical values, which will be developed and explored throughout this series: sharing love, shaping lives, serving, and sending.

In your life, having discovered Christ, you no doubt are finding that you want to grow in your knowledge of him. You want to shape your life according to his Word to be his disciple. As you do, you will discover a personal ministry, a way to use your spiritual gifts to serve others. Then, having been filled with compassion for others, you will be moved to go out into the world beyond your church walls, fulfilling the Great Commission by making new disciples, thus completing the cycle of discipleship.

THE PROCESS: BUILDING DEEPER FAITH

The aim of the Building Deeper Faith series is to form disciples according to the Great Commandment and the Great Commission. The construction process of such faith can be organized around five categories: (1) foundational truths, (2) life practices, (3) virtues, (4) core values, and (5) mission.

Foundational Truths

Building Deeper Faith is based on foundational truths that are key elements for life transformation. These biblical concepts encompass the scope of Christian thinking and are always at the heart of Christian love. Learning these concepts and how they help us love God and our neighbors well will help us grow in our faith.

Life Practices

All believers must move from theory to practice. That is, we must learn to apply biblical truth to life. The practices identified in Building Deeper Faith will help us see and become open to God's work in and through us, providing the evidence of the change he is making in our lives.

Virtues

Virtues are Christlike qualities that emerge in the lives of those who are alive in Christ. Virtues replace thoughts and attitudes that come all too naturally to us whenever we are living independently from God—that is, when we are living in sin. The virtues that God's Spirit creates in us (also known in Scripture as the fruit of the Spirit) reveal the developing character into which he is transforming us, and it is what God's Spirit uses to attract others to Christ.

Core Values

Biblical truth must be applied in the framework of Christ's body, the church. The core values are the guiding principles by which the church should function in love. They are our method of operating lovingly toward God and our neighbors—they describe how and why we do the things we do.

Mission

Ultimately, believers called to love are to serve. Our mission describes what it is that we do for Christ. Each biblical truth finds a practical expression in our work.

YOUR INVOLVEMENT: SPIRITUAL DISCIPLINES

Growing disciples discover something exciting and transformational in Christian worship. The worship service is the point of entry to most churches. Yet as important as worship is, believers need more in order to grow deeper in their faith. In fact, we all long for deeper relationships.

Wouldn't it be great if there were a place we could go to make friends and find answers? Wouldn't it be wonderful if we could discover a forum to open our hearts, grow in the faith, and find unconditional love?

There is such a place—your study group!

Discipleship groups provide exactly what is needed for building deeper faith. This is because discipleship goes far beyond knowledge or even worship—it can only be meaningful as God designed in the context of loving relationships.

Just as the New Testament church was built up on teaching and preaching (Acts 5:42), so today's church must be built up by Bible study. But the key is that faith is gained. Knowledge that builds faith is ideally found in fellowship with other believers. Being connected to spiritual family as we learn makes a world of difference between mere academic knowledge acquisition and authentic discipleship.

Every believer needs a protected environment in which to discover and practice his or her faith. If you want to grow and become more effective in Christ, then find and commit to a discipleship group in which you can grow in him.

Within the context of a discipleship group, there are several simple disciplines that God's Spirit often uses powerfully in the spiritual formation of his people. Consider just these few disciplines as you seek to grow deeper in your love for God through the study of this book.

Bible Reading and Study

The Building Deeper Faith series is designed to direct you to the Bible at every point in your study. Each chapter begins with a few important Scripture passages and includes several Bible references to explore. You can enhance your study by using a good Bible translation, written in today's language.

Scripture Memorization

Memorization is a simple way to gain ownership of important passages. Each of the chapters in this book includes a key verse to memorize. This too-often-ignored discipline is a powerful tool to help you gain confidence in your knowledge of Scripture and in hearing God speak to you.

Daily Prayer and Reflection

Time alone with God is perhaps the single most important spiritual practice for any disciple. Try to spend time in prayer and reflection every day.

Personal Spiritual Journal Writing

Journal writing is a way to enhance time spent in prayer and reflection. Recording observations about your life and faith will help you process what you are learning and clarify the spiritual issues in your life. Take this study as your opportunity to begin the practice of journal writing. You'll be glad you did.

May God richly bless you and draw you closer in knowledge and love for him as you study and fellowship together with his people in your pursuit of authentic discipleship by building deeper faith.

REALIZE THE DEPTHS OF SALVATION

Salvation is found in no one else, for there is no other name under heaven given to mankind by which we must be saved.

—Acts 4:12

BIBLE BASICS

- Acts 16:29–31
- John 3:3
- John 3:16
- Romans 5:1–2
- Titus 3:5

Reflect on your experience of coming to know Christ as your personal Savior. Write a brief account of your own salvation.

OUR NEED FOR SALVATION

The Bible is a book of salvation. While it speaks of many things, including prophets and kings, laws and covenants, miracles and mysteries, it is not primarily a history book. It is really a book about how we can be saved by God's grace.

But who needs to be saved? Do *we* need to be saved? If so, why?

First Corinthians 15:3 declares that "Christ died for our sins in accordance with the Scriptures" (ESV). The fact that Christ died is an easily verified historical reality. When we say, however, that Christ *died for our sins*, we're speaking of something more than a historical fact. If Christ *died for us*, his death becomes personal; it has implications for everyone. Christ's death on the cross was not a human tragedy; it was an act of deliverance! We needed help, and God sent his Son to our rescue.

But we've gotten ahead of ourselves. If Christ died for us, there must be a reason. And to discover that reason, we must travel all the way back to the beginning.

The Problem of Sin

When God created Adam and Eve, the first two people in the world, he was pleased with his creation. It was pure and good. But Satan tempted our first parents to eat from the Tree of Knowledge of Good and Evil, an act God had forbidden. Satan convinced them that if they ate the fruit of the tree, then they would be like God. So they ate, and therefore sinned. Immediately they fell from God's favor and were expelled from the garden of Eden.

As you think about your own life, isn't it true that a tug-of-war is going on within you? At times you want to do what is right, but at other times you want to do what is wrong. Perhaps in the past you wanted to obey your parents or others in authority over you, even God, but at other times you wanted to break free and do your own thing.

In what ways did you rebel against God before you became a Christian?

The Effect of the Fall

Adam and Eve tried to live without God. When they sinned, they lost some, though not all, of the divine image. Since we are Adam and Eve's offspring, we lost a great deal when they fell. We are neither what we ought to be nor what we were meant to be. Apart from Christ, we live in rebellion against God. At times we want to be good, but we fail to measure up to God's high standard of righteousness. Romans 3:10 says, "There is none righteous, not even one" (NASB).

First Corinthians 15:22 says, "In Adam all die." All people are born in sin. Sin is not just an action, but also a state of being. We are born into a sinful condition, and our sinful acts are an expression of that condition. The image of God within us was damaged when our first parents sinned. In other words, we are both good and bad. We do have some good thoughts and good desires, but our sin has separated us from God. We are trapped in a life of habitual disobedience.

We all need salvation. We need to come back to God. We need God's forgiveness and a right relationship with him.

Look at the world. It's obvious that something is wrong. Races hate each other, husbands and wives turn against each another, people are addicted to alcohol and drugs, and people rape and murder.

What's wrong with the world?

The answer is sin. Something must be done to deal with it.

What evidence of sin do you see in your community? Your workplace? Yourself?

Our Desire for Salvation

It seems everyone wants salvation. People in every land reach out for rescue from sin. Though they might not call their desperate condition *sin*, they recognize a problem in the world and in themselves. Everyone longs to be someone else. Some call this longing a quest for freedom. Others describe it as a desire to be a better person. Still others think of it as a desire to be safe—to be delivered from the fear of death.

We see this longing for salvation in the Old Testament. There the children of Israel thought of salvation as being safe or victorious. At the time of the exodus, deliverance from Egypt was a form of salvation by God. In fact, Moses said to the children of Israel: "Do not be afraid. Stand firm and you will see the deliverance the LORD will bring you today" (Ex. 14:13).

In the centuries before Christ, and even during Christ's earthly ministry, people sought political deliverance, but they despaired of seeing that salvation in their time. Life was difficult, because much evil and hatred permeated the world. Rulers terribly oppressed people, and many people lived in slavery. They longed for deliverance, but they did not believe it would come.

Later, when Christ came to earth, some Jews saw him as their deliverer. They believed he would save them from the Roman Empire's domination. They later rejected Christ, largely because he did not turn out to be a political deliverer. They were looking for national salvation, not the personal, spiritual deliverance he offered.

To this day, people are seeking a savior. Some look to politics, psychology, medicine, other sciences, or economics. Others still refuse to believe that salvation is even possible. But all are longing for a savior and a solution to the problem of sin.

In what ways did you look for salvation? What were you running from? What were you running toward?

GOD'S PLAN FOR US

The first few chapters of Genesis give the story of creation and the sad account of humankind's fall from fellowship with God. But the rest of the Bible relates God's plan to restore that fellowship. It's a wonderful story of God's mighty acts as he worked to solve the problems caused by sin. It is the story of salvation.

The story begins in the Old Testament, when God began to work through people like Abraham, Moses, and the prophets. It continues in the New Testament, which records how God came to earth through his Son, Jesus Christ, to deliver us from sin.

Let's trace the steps that God took in making salvation available to each of us.

Preparation

The fall of humankind did not catch God off guard. He knew everything from the beginning. That does not mean, however, that God determined that Adam and Eve would sin. It simply means that even before they sinned, he knew what their actions would be and what would result from those actions. He had already developed a plan to restore all people to himself. Revelation 13:8 identifies Christ as the "Lamb slain from the foundation of the world" (KJV). God anticipated that, when given the choice, Adam and Eve would choose to sin. And he was prepared to offer his Son, the Lamb of God, as the perfect sacrifice on behalf of all humanity.

Incarnation: Christ's Birth

When Jesus was born in Bethlehem, as related in the wonderful Christmas story, God became one of us. Christ Jesus was God, and he became a man "born of a woman, born under the law" (Gal. 4:4).

This is a great mystery and wonderful miracle. Christ was fully God, without sin, the perfect One to die for our sins. At the same time, he was fully human. That baby in the manger really was the Son of God, and yet he was just like any other baby. He cried, was hungry, needed his mother, and had other wants and needs. He was 100 percent God *and* completely human.

The Cross: Christ's Death

Jesus lived on earth for about thirty-three years. For three years, he traveled throughout ancient Palestine preaching the good news and performing great miracles. Finally, the authorities of his day rejected him and put him to death on a cross.

The cross is central to our salvation because it provided the remedy for sin. Although it was a cruel injustice in human terms, the cross was part of God's plan to save the world. Paul wrote in 2 Corinthians 5:19, "God was reconciling the world to himself in Christ."

Because he was both God and man, Jesus could touch God with one hand and us with the other. When he died on the cross, his arms were outstretched. He reached to God and to us. And by dying for us, he made it possible for God and us to be brought together. This is called the *reconciliation* (see Rom. 5:9–11).

Did Christ *have* to die in order to reconcile us to God? If so, why?

According to God's plan, there can be no forgiveness for sin without bloodshed. Leviticus 17:11 states, "For the life of a creature is in the blood, and I have given it to you to make atonement for yourselves on the altar; it is the blood that makes atonement for one's life." In Old Testament times, people received God's forgiveness through the slaughter of a lamb. The lamb's blood symbolized life for the person offering the sacrifice.

Also, during the Passover, when the children of Israel left Egypt, a lamb's blood was splashed on the doorframe of every home, symbolizing that a death had taken place. That symbolic act meant salvation for the ancient Israelites, and it looked forward to the day when Christ would die on the cross for us.

By his death—specifically by shedding his blood—Christ provided salvation for all who believe in him.

The Resurrection: Christ's New Life

Christ's resurrection is all-important. Without the resurrection, we would have no reason to believe, no hope, and no salvation. Why is the resurrection so vital in the plan of salvation?

The resurrection vindicates Jesus. The Jews thought he was a pretender, and at times even his own disciples doubted him. But the resurrection proved that Jesus really is God's Son. Peter preached on the day of Pentecost, "Let all Israel be assured of this: God has made this Jesus, whom you crucified, both Lord and Christ" (Acts 2:36).

The resurrection also declares God's triumph over the forces of sin and death. So the apostle Paul could write with full confidence, "'Death has been swallowed up in victory. Where, O death, is your victory? Where, O death, is your sting?' The sting of death is sin, and the power of sin is the law. But thanks be to God! He gives us the victory through our Lord Jesus Christ" (1 Cor. 15:54–57).

The fact that Jesus rose from the dead is what gives us hope for an eternal life. Because Jesus rose, we know that we will rise too.

The Ascension: Christ's Return to the Father

The ascension of Christ into heaven is recorded in Acts 1:9: "After he said this, he was taken up before their very eyes, and a cloud hid him from their sight." The ascension placed Christ at his rightful place—at God the Father's right hand. This event relates to our salvation in three ways:

1. Exaltation: The Father exalted Christ. He lifted him up all the way from the grave to his right hand (see Eph. 4:8–9).
2. Intercession: Christ is at the Father's right hand right now, interceding on our behalf (see Rom. 8:34; 1 John 2:1).
3. Advocation: Jesus promised that after he was gone, the Advocate would come to us. His promise was fulfilled by the pouring out of the Holy Spirit upon Christ's followers (see Acts 2:33; John 15:26; 16:7).

The Second Coming: Christ's Return

Christ's return is the final act in our salvation. The Bible promises, "This same Jesus, who has been taken from you into heaven, will come back in the same way you have seen him go into heaven" (Acts 1:11). We have already been delivered from the guilt, power, and penalty of sin through faith in Christ Jesus. Our redemption will be realized when we've passed into eternity, as well as when Christ returns and delivers humanity from the physical effects of sin.

Salvation involves not only individuals, but also the whole world. God has permitted Satan to exercise some power over human history, but God will not allow that to continue forever. God will one day take the reins of human governments in his hand, and his will shall be done on earth even as it is done in heaven. If it were not for Christ's final return, our redemption would be forever incomplete.

THE STEPS CHRIST TOOK TO SAVE US

- Incarnation—his birth
- Cross—his death
- Resurrection—his life
- Ascension—his return to the Father
- Second Coming—his return

What new ideas about God's plan for salvation have you learned from this chapter?

RECEIVING CHRIST JESUS AS SAVIOR

We know why we need salvation—because sin entered the world when Adam and Eve sinned in the garden of Eden. We inherited their sinful nature that keeps us from being in a right relationship with God. And we know what Christ did to provide salvation—he came to earth as a baby, died on the cross, rose from the dead, ascended into heaven—and he will come again.

Since you are reading this book, it's likely that you have already realized your need for forgiveness and have reached out to God, accepting his gift of salvation. Now here's a big question: Exactly what happened when you were saved?

God's First Step: Grace

It's important to remember that salvation does not begin with us; it begins with God. Before you ever asked for God's forgiveness, his Holy Spirit drew you to him.

That action on God's part—that work of the Holy Spirit that turned your heart toward God—is called *prevenient grace* (or *initial grace*). This grace precedes salvation. It prepares our hearts to meet God and enables us to respond when he offers forgiveness.

In Titus 2:11, we read, "For the grace of God has appeared that offers salvation to all people." Grace is a gift. At the very beginning of the salvation process, God offers us a gift. It is a gift of love. He loves you. He loves everybody.

You have experienced this initial grace of God. Think of the times a song, an experience, or a feeling of love or even sadness moved you to feel sorry for your sins and reach out to God. Perhaps there was a time when you said to yourself, "I should live a different life," "I should start attending church," or "I should get my life in order." Thoughts like these are evidence of God's work in you. The Holy Spirit prompted those thoughts so you might open your heart to God and his will for you.

That's grace.

Your First Step: Faith

Salvation depends entirely upon God making the first move toward you—*prevenient grace*. But God does not force salvation on anyone. Each of us has free will. We may choose to believe in him, or we may choose not to believe.

If we are to be saved, we must believe.

Most people begin by believing historical things about God. For example, they believe that he created the world or that he sent his Son, Jesus, to die on the cross. They may accept the fact that Jesus was a real person or that he also died on the cross or that the resurrection actually happened.

Think about your journey to faith in Christ. What were the first things you believed about him? How strongly did you believe them? Which beliefs did you struggle with?

To be saved, a person must move beyond accepting the facts about God, although that is where faith begins (see Heb. 11:6). Saving faith is the act of believing what God did in Christ for you personally.

On one occasion, a jailer asked the apostle Paul, "What must I do to be saved?" Paul answered, "Believe in the Lord Jesus" (Acts 16:30–31).

Belief is an action. We must choose to accept the gospel message as truth, and we must act on that choice by accepting it personally. Faith involves both an inward act of believing "with your heart" and an outward act of confession "with your mouth" (Rom. 10:8–10).

A time came when you took this first step in the process of salvation. Once you made the choice to believe, your faith was strengthened by additional knowledge. Christ Jesus, your new friend, entered your life and now helps you grow. He wants you to keep on growing throughout your entire life. You have embarked on the lifelong journey of faith.

Sorrow for Sin: Repentance

Genuine faith in Christ always includes a turning away from sin. That's called *repentance*. Both John the Baptist and Jesus began their ministries with a call to repentance (see Matt. 3:2; 4:17), and this call to repentance was at the heart of Jesus' mission (see Luke 5:32).

To repent means to change one's mind. That change includes both our opinions and our intentions. Many people who have done wrong are sorry they were caught or sorry they had to suffer because of it. That is not repentance. Repentance includes two things: a confession of sin (see Matt. 3:6; Mark 1:5) and a determination to change (see Luke 3:4–14).

If there is no change in our lives, it's likely that we didn't really repent and believe in Christ. While faith alone is the condition of our salvation, the kind of faith that is necessary for salvation is faith that has a spirit of humility, of repentance. Without repentance, faith is merely intellectual assent; it is not a personal acceptance of God's grace. You might say that repentance is the evidence of our faith—it demonstrates that our belief in Christ is genuine.

Do you recall being sorry for your sins? What changes have taken place in your life as a result of your new faith?

WHAT HAPPENS WHEN YOU ARE SAVED?

What happens when a person believes in Christ? The end of all true belief is salvation, or "being saved" from sin.

Sin has a claim on the sinner, and it bothers the conscience, separating the person from God. We cannot hide from God, and we cannot reform our lives to appease God. Only one hope is offered to us: forgiveness.

Forgiveness

Those who believe in Jesus are forgiven. The Bible says, "If we confess our sins, he is faithful and just and will forgive us our sins and purify us from all unrighteousness" (1 John 1:9). We can infer the same from Jesus' own words in John 8:24: "I told you that you would die in your sins; if you do not believe that I am he, you will indeed die in your sins."

When we believe in Christ and repent of our sins, God forgives us. Forgiveness is the initial experience of salvation.

Justification or Pardon

Can we who are born as sinful people ever be truly justified before God? Yes, we can be.

Luke 18:10–14 relates the story of a truly repentant man. Having confessed his sin to God, "he went down to his house justified" (KJV). How was that possible?

Since we have sinned, we are guilty before God. But when God forgives us, he pardons us and makes us acceptable in his sight. Since Jesus took our guilt upon himself and paid the price for our sin, we may receive this pardon.

Perhaps you can think of a time when you were guilty of doing something wrong. You may have tried to justify your actions by making excuses or blaming others, but in your heart, you know that it didn't work. You couldn't pardon yourself.

But when you asked God for forgiveness, a miracle took place. God, who alone can forgive sins, really did forgive you and make you "right" with him.

It is a wonderful thing to be justified before God. Now you are not condemned. You have God's favor. You have been delivered from the guilt, penalty, and slavery of sin. No longer do you stand before the judge as a convicted criminal. Instead, you have a new relationship with God. You have been reconciled with him. As the Bible says, "We have peace with God through our Lord Jesus Christ" (Rom. 5:1).

The New Birth: Regeneration

Recall that when Adam and Eve fell, the image of God within them—and within us—was damaged. By regeneration, we are restored to a new likeness of God and to a new relationship with him.

In order for us to become God's children, a supernatural change must occur. We must be born again. This new birth—called *regeneration*—is not a second physical birth, but a birth of spiritual life. "I came that they may have life, and have it abundantly," Jesus declared (John 10:10 NASB). This new life is a refreshing, cleansed, renewed life in the Spirit. Jesus said, "Whoever hears my word and believes him who sent me has eternal life and will not be judged but has crossed over from death to life" (John 5:24).

WHAT HAPPENS IN SALVATION

Prevenient Grace	The Holy Spirit draws us to God.
Faith	We choose to accept God's grace.
Repentance	We are sorry for sin and turn from it.
Forgiveness	God forgives our sin.
Justification or Pardon	We are made right with God.
Regeneration	We are born again, made alive in Christ.
Adoption	We are included in God's family.
Assurance	God's Spirit confirms that we are saved.
Initial Sanctification	God begins the process of cleansing our hearts.

Salvation is not simply deliverance from the threat of eternal damnation; it is salvation to a new life now—a life that pleases God and that is pleasing to us. We are Christians not simply because we want to go to heaven, but because the Christian life is the most satisfying, fullest, and most joyful life one can possibly live. In fact, it is life as God intended it to be when he created human beings in the first place!

Adoption as a Child of God

Adoption is the act of receiving a stranger into the family and giving that person all the rights and privileges belonging to a natural child. Adoption is also a result of salvation. When you are saved, you are adopted into God's family.

The supreme right that Christ gives to those who take him as Savior and Lord is the right to become *children of God* (see John 1:12). God created us, so we already have a relationship with him as created ones to the Creator. But one result of salvation is that we may enter a new relationship with God, one as child to Father. When we believe in Jesus Christ, we become God's children with all the privileges he bestows on his children.

All of these things—forgiveness, justification, regeneration, and adoption—happen at the same time. However, while *justification* is a legal term, *adoption* is a relational term. It implies more than pardon for sin; it expresses a covenant relationship. The Bible says, "God sent his Son, born of a woman, born under the law, to redeem those under the law, that we might receive adoption to sonship" (Gal. 4:4–5). And "to all who did receive him, to those who believed in his name, he gave the right to become children of God" (John 1:12).

Since you have repented of your sins and believed in Christ, you are truly a child of God. "The Spirit you received does not make you slaves, so that you live in fear again; rather, the Spirit you received brought about your adoption to sonship. And by him we cry, 'Abba, Father.' The Spirit himself testifies with our spirit that we are God's children" (Rom. 8:15–16).

Which aspect of salvation is most meaningful to you? Why?

KNOWING THAT YOU ARE SAVED

Have you been saved from sin? How do you know? Can you be sure that you are now a member of God's family?

Yes, you can be certain. You don't need to guess whether or not you've been forgiven and have eternal life. You have the assurance of God's presence and approval.

Here are two experiences that are evidences of our salvation.

The Witness of the Spirit

The Holy Spirit will reward a believer's search for assurance of salvation by a divine perception. This is more than human intuition; it is direct divine illumination. The Holy Spirit creates an awareness within us that we have accepted Christ and that he has accepted us. Our faith leads to "peace with God" (Rom. 5:1).

Nations know when they are fighting and when they are at peace. So it is with our relationship with God. We know when we are at war with him, and we know when the battle is over. "The Spirit himself testifies with our spirit" (Rom. 8:16). This assurance is not secondhand; it is an inner, personal persuasion created by the Holy Spirit himself.

This persuasion is deeper than an intellectual understanding. Frankly, no one can explain how this "testimony by the Spirit" is made apparent to the heart, but it is. The Holy Spirit gives every believer an assurance of his or her adoption by God.

Awareness of Change

Those who have been born again know they are different from what they were. They can each say, "Something has happened to me. I'm not the person I was." Salvation brings a religious and moral change in us. We have a new attitude toward God, and we become alive to spiritual things. Also, there is a moral difference in the way we live; we make choices based on a new set of standards.

Some observable evidences of this change are that we have a new determination to obey God, that we make a radical break with the old life, and that we have our lives reoriented toward God and spiritual things.

So then, we know that we have peace with God both by the inner witness of the Spirit and by honest self-examination. As the Bible says, "Examine yourselves to see whether you are in the faith; test yourselves. Do you not realize that Christ Jesus is in you—unless, of course, you fail the test?" (2 Cor. 13:5).

What changes have you seen in your life since you accepted Christ into your heart?

WHAT COMES NEXT?

Knowing that you are a Christian brings a wonderful sense of peace. But God did not save us in order to leave us where we are. He has a plan for each of our lives, and that plan includes our growth as individuals and our service to him.

Initial Sanctification

The kingdom of God, according to Paul, is "righteousness, peace and joy in the Holy Spirit" (Rom. 14:17). Christ bore our sins, not as a substitute for our righteousness, but "that we might die to sins and live for righteousness" (1 Pet. 2:24). God intends for us to actually live a new and different life after we're saved. It is God's intention to make us holy through and through (see 1 Thess. 5:23).

When we were born again, the Spirit created a new life in us. We were changed, cleansed, made holy. But that cleansing is a continuing work of God's Holy Spirit in our lives. Holiness is not what we accomplish, but rather it is what God's Holy Spirit is completing in us so that we are not in the least separated from him. (Separation from God is the cause of all that is sin.) This is the only way we can become holy and separated from all uncleanliness: independence from sin can only happen as we are united with God in love. He promises to accomplish sanctification in us entirely by the work of his Holy Spirit in us. That process begins at the moment of our new birth. Self-centeredness is still present to some degree, even in a person who has been born again. The uncleanness acquired through years of living apart from Christ is real, but we receive an initial cleansing, or sanctification, the moment we are saved.

Remember, it was a process of God's grace that led you to repentance and faith in Christ. That process never ends. God's work of making you holy has begun in you, but in the future, you'll face significant experiences that will bring a deeper cleansing in your life. What he has begun in you, he will continue throughout all of your life if you remain obedient to him.

Witnessing

If a man staggered into your room and warned you that the building would be blown up in five minutes, what would you do? It's possible that you might thank him for the information, tell him you believed him, and then quickly show him to the door. If you were still in the building five minutes later, however, he could rightly conclude that you really had not believed him at all.

Likewise, you might claim to believe that Jesus Christ is the Savior of the world, that life's full meaning can be realized only through him, and that apart from him all people are under the threat of eternal damnation. But if you continue to live as before, never telling anyone the good news of salvation, nobody would put much stock in your claim.

FIVE PRINCIPLES FOR WITNESSING

Cultivate Social Contacts	Make a conscious effort to be with non-Christians. Witnessing to church folk will not win the lost.
Establish a Common Interest	Begin where their interests lie. Spiritual matters need not be the first subject of conversation.
Don't Condemn	Be a good listener. Understanding a nonbeliever is not the same as condoning his or her behavior.
Stick with the Main Issue	Refuse to be sidetracked by controversial issues. Focus on the truth of the gospel.
Confront Directly	At some point, present the claims of Christ and challenge the nonbeliever to make a decision. Saving faith, not mere friendship, is the goal.

If we genuinely believe the gospel, nonbelievers will see a commitment to that truth in our everyday living. People who do not know Christ need to see the reality of genuine Christian experience in our lives. Only then will our words about Jesus Christ persuade them to know him personally.

Perhaps the best way to tell others about salvation is to relate your own experience. You can witness—share your faith with others—simply by telling them what God did in your life through Jesus Christ.

And witnessing goes beyond what we say. It includes all that we are and, therefore, all that we do. When you live your life for Christ, others will notice your example. As you are faithful to him, your life will serve as a witness to the good news.

Have you told anyone about your new faith in Jesus Christ? Who is the first (or next) person with whom you will share the good news about salvation?

KNOW GOD THROUGH HIS WORD

All Scripture is God-breathed and is useful for teaching, rebuking, correcting and training in righteousness, so that the servant of God may be thoroughly equipped for every good work.

—2 Timothy 3:16–17

BIBLE BASICS

- 2 Timothy 3:14–17

What uses of the Bible do you see in the passage above? List some ways you use the Bible in your church and personal life.

A UNIQUE BOOK

The Bible is a unique book. There is nothing like it for helping us know God and understand how to please him. The apostle Paul gave the Bible the highest possible affirmation when he called it "God-breathed."

He stated that it had the noble task of preparing God's people to declare the gospel. He couldn't have been more right. Nothing else does for us what the Bible does. When necessary, it touches those areas of our lives that disappoint our heavenly Father. In fact, it does more than touch; it can slice like a scalpel to remove sin from our lives.

The Bible was one of the first books to be printed, and it remains the best-selling book of all time. In this chapter, we will learn why Paul believed it was inspired, and we'll trace its fascinating development from the ancient world to your hands. Then we'll discover how you can get the most from the Bible so that you, too, will be "thoroughly equipped for every good work."

HOW WE KNOW THE BIBLE IS TRUE

To say that the Bible is God-breathed is an astounding claim. The term *God-breathed* (or *inspired*) conjures up an image of God breathing life into the Book as he did into Adam at creation. This means God was ultimately responsible for producing the Book, and it continues to have relevance unlike some books that become obsolete soon after they are published. To say that the Bible is God-breathed implies that it will always be true and effective.

When Paul claimed all Scripture was God-breathed, he was talking about the Old Testament, the first thirty-nine books of the Bible. Several things brought him to this conclusion.

Why We Trust the Old Testament

In Paul's day, the Old Testament was the Bible of the Jews. The Jews are a race chosen by God about two thousand years before the time of

Christ. God revealed himself to them many times and in various ways. The Jews wrote down what God said and did. They believed what they were writing was not merely their own interpretation of God's words and actions, but was an inspired account of who he is. Over a span of nearly a thousand years, the Jews collected these writings and used them as their Bible.

The Words Came from God

The first leader of the Jews, Moses, gave God's chosen people many instructions, including the Ten Commandments. He made it clear that the commands were not his but God's. Prophets like Moses often introduced their messages with the phrase, "This is what the LORD says." According to the Jews, the books of the Bible that do not specifically claim inspiration have demonstrated their divine origin in other ways; they contain fulfilled prophecies or agree with books known to be inspired.

Some books were recognized as inspired soon after they were written. The Israelites understood immediately that they must obey the commands God gave through Moses. Daniel understood that Jeremiah's prophecies came from God. Acceptance of some books as divinely inspired took longer, but the Old Testament was essentially complete by about 100 BC.

It Was Accepted by Early Christians

The very first Christians were Jewish, so they used the Old Testament as their Bible. As the church grew, it included people who were not Jewish (called *Gentiles*). They, too, accepted the Old Testament as their Bible. After all, Jesus had considered the Old Testament to be inspired. When Jesus' enemies confronted him, he turned to the Old Testament for his definitive answers (see Matt. 4:1–11; Mark 7:1–13).

All the authors of the New Testament books shared Jesus' high view of the Old Testament. Peter said, "The word of the LORD endures forever" (1 Pet. 1:25).

It's a Completely Reliable Book

The Old Testament has a unity that human beings could not have created. Although the books come from many different authors with many different perspectives, purposes, and styles, all of them agree on who God is and what he is doing.

Many Old Testament predictions were later shown to have been fulfilled. For example, it was predicted that the Jews would become slaves in Egypt but later be liberated and receive the land of Canaan. Those events took place several hundred years after the prediction was made. It was also predicted that the Jews would go into exile because of their disobedience but would receive permission from King Cyrus to return home. Again, these events happened exactly as predicted.

Early Christians also noticed that certain events in their own day had been predicted in the Old Testament. The prophets said that the Savior would be born to a virgin in Bethlehem, that he would proclaim the good news about what God was doing, enter Jerusalem in triumph, be betrayed by a friend, and be killed for our sins. Jesus' life and ministry fulfilled each of those predictions. And on more than one occasion, Jesus stated that the Old Testament had spoken about him (see Luke 24:13–35).

WHY WE TRUST THE NEW TESTAMENT

For the first several decades after Jesus' ministry on earth, the early Christians were content to use the Old Testament as their Bible.

However, as the church spread, leaders like Paul wrote letters to the Christians for whom they had responsibility. These letters were collected and treasured, and copies were circulated among the churches.

Eventually, accounts of Jesus' life were also collected, written down, and circulated. We know these collections as the Gospels. Luke, one of Paul's associates, wrote a sequel to his gospel in which he recorded the history of the early church. This sequel was called the Acts of the Apostles (usually shortened to Acts). Together, these books came to be regarded as inspired, just as the Old Testament was, and became known as the New Testament, to which more books were added later.

It Was Selected by Early Christians

As with the Old Testament, the books for the New Testament were selected based on the collective opinion of God's people over a long period of time. First, the early Christians wanted to know whether a book was written by an apostle or his associate. Then they carefully considered what it said. Was it true? Did it contain fulfilled prophecies? Did it agree with other books already considered inspired?

Within about two hundred years after Jesus' time, the church had agreed that the twenty-seven books of the New Testament were inspired. About two hundred years later that decision became official. Since then, Christians have agreed that both the Old Testament and New Testament are "God-breathed."

It Has Internal and External Confirmations

All available evidence confirms the early church's decision. No other book can match the Bible's content in unity and truth. No other book can boast so many fulfilled prophecies. No other book has accomplished what the Bible has.

To make the matter even more certain, God puts his stamp of approval on the Bible. He does this for each one of us in our hearts by his Holy Spirit. We recognize the Bible's truthfulness when God applies it to our lives, teaching and correcting us, training us to be godly people. When you have experienced God personally applying his Word to your life, you will understand for yourself that it is true.

REASONS TO BELIEVE THE BIBLE IS INSPIRED

1. It claims to be inspired.
2. Jesus said it is inspired.
3. Its prophecies have been fulfilled.
4. Its message is consistent throughout all books.
5. It has had a great impact on civilization.
6. The Holy Spirit reveals to us that it is inspired.

Do most people you know think God inspired the Bible? Why or why not? Do you believe it is divinely inspired? Why or why not?

WHY THE BIBLE IS IMPORTANT

The Bible profoundly impacts our lives for at least four reasons.

It Is God's Word

First, God has spoken through this Book. Other books might tell the truth, but only one communicates all the truth we need in order to know God and lead a godly life. We can confidently form our understanding of God from what we learn in the Bible. It is the only authorized biography of God, his autobiography!

Also, the Bible enables us to form unchanging standards of right and wrong. It accurately relates the history of the universe, humanity, and how God brought salvation to the world. It describes the future and gives an accurate view of who we are. Many books have been written about people, but only one has been written by their Creator.

God Continues to Speak through It

Since God inspired the Bible, he *still* speaks through it to his people. When you read this chapter, you will "hear" the author speaking to you, but with significant limitations. The author will not be present when you read these words and not able to personally speak to you.

When you read the Bible, God can speak directly to you through his Holy Spirit. You may not hear him every time you open the Bible, and you shouldn't expect to hear an audible voice. If you listen, however, God will apply his Word to you personally. He may want to teach you something. He may rebuke and correct you for some shortcoming. Or he may train you to become more righteous. Because the Bible is God's Word, it still speaks to those who listen.

It Is a Training Tool for Christians

If you are a follower of God, then you are serious about obeying his commands. Learning lessons from God is similar to learning lessons at school—instruction is never easy! But as sincere followers of God, we humble ourselves and accept God's instruction, correction, and rebuke. Since the Bible is God's Word to us, it is our primary training tool, and we accept its message, even when it's challenging.

It Is God's Gift to Us

If a famous person or world leader sent you a personal letter, would you need to be prodded to read it? Of course not! You would probably tear open the envelope and carefully read every word. We have received an even more precious gift—God has sent us a message. Not only that, but he comes along with it to help us better understand it. We should eagerly read and study the Bible to learn what he has to say.

Describe a time when you felt that God was speaking to you through the Bible.

HOW WE GOT THE BIBLE

Since the Bible is God's Word, we want to understand it thoroughly. Reading the Bible can be intimidating, however. It's a very long book. The events described in it took place a long time ago and in faraway lands, and the plot can be difficult to follow. That's why it's helpful to understand something about the Bible's background—how it was written and how it came to be in its present form.

Original Writings

Most of the Old Testament was written in the Hebrew language of the ancient Jews. About three centuries before the time of Christ, the Old Testament was translated into Greek to make it available to Jews who no longer spoke Hebrew. This translation, known as the *Septuagint*, was the version of the Bible that Jesus and the early Christians used. Later, the New Testament, also written in Greek, was added to the Septuagint. Together, these books were circulated as the Christian

Bible. Since the printing press had not yet been invented, all copies of the Bible were handwritten.

As the news about Jesus spread to other countries, it became necessary to translate the Bible into languages such as Latin, Syriac, and Coptic. With the development of the printing press in the 1400s, manuscripts could be mass-produced quickly and less expensively than before.

MAJOR TRANSLATIONS OF THE BIBLE

Version	Date
Septuagint (Greek Old Testament)	200–400 BC
Vulgate (Latin Bible)	AD 300–400
Luther's German Bible	1534
Tyndale's New Testament and Pentateuch	1530
Geneva Bible	1560
King James	1611
American Standard	1901
Revised Standard	1952
New American Standard	1971
Living Bible (paraphrase)	1971
New International	1978
Good News	1979
New King James	1982
The Message (paraphrase)	1994
Contemporary English	1995
New Living	1996
New English	2005

Eventually, new translations became necessary not only so the Bible could be read in new languages, but also so it could continue to be understood in languages that had changed over time. This was why the king of England authorized a new translation in 1611, which came to be known as the King James Version. New translations have been appearing in English and other languages ever since.

Many Translations

Translating any ancient book into a modern language is tricky. It is often impossible to find a word in the modern language that matches the original word exactly. Also, the meaning of any word depends heavily on the context in which it is used, but the context of the ancient writings is not always easy to determine.

The meaning of some languages, including English, depends heavily on the order of words in sentences. That is not the case for Greek and Hebrew. Translators face another problem with idioms and figures of speech. Should they be translated literally or not?

So many different translations of the Bible exist, in part, because people have different opinions about how to translate an ancient book. Some people believe a translation should match the original language as closely as possible, including exact matches of word meanings, precise retention of word order, and literal renderings for figures of speech. These highly literal translations are more exact, but they are also more difficult to understand.

Other translators believe it is more important to represent the author's intended meaning rather than to translate every word precisely. These translators might change the word order to parallel English usage more closely or substitute a figure of speech that is more common in our language. These translations are less precise, but they probably do a better job conveying a passage's overall meaning to the average reader. Versions of this type are sometimes called paraphrases.

Still a third group of translators use a method known as dynamic equivalence. This method aims to balance the literal and paraphrase approaches. The result is a translation that is more readable than a literal translation but more exact than a paraphrase.

To illustrate the three types of translation, here are three versions of 1 Samuel 20:30.

1 SAMUEL 20:30		
Translation Theory	Version	Text
Literal	English Standard Version	Then Saul's anger was kindled against Jonathan, and he said to him, "You son of a perverse, rebellious woman, do I not know that you have chosen the son of Jesse to your own shame, and to the shame of your mother's nakedness?"
Paraphrase	Contemporary English Version	Saul was furious with Jonathan and yelled, "You're no son of mine, you traitor! I know you've chosen to be loyal to that son of Jesse. You should be ashamed of yourself! And your own mother should be ashamed that you were ever born."
Dynamic Equivalence	New International Version	Saul's anger flared up at Jonathan and he said to him, "You son of a perverse and rebellious woman! Don't I know that you have sided with the son of Jesse to your own shame and to the shame of the mother who bore you?"

The first is a more literal translation of the original Hebrew but is harder to understand. The second is very easy to understand. While not a word-for-word translation, it represents exactly what Saul was saying and the shock value he intended. The third translation strikes a balance between the two.

Choosing the Right Translation

As you can see, each type of translation has advantages and disadvantages. Each provides something the others lack. Which one is right for you? It depends. If you are reading the Bible for the first time, choose a paraphrase, since it will be easy to understand. For daily reading, a dynamic equivalence translation is probably best. If you are studying the Bible in-depth, you may prefer the accuracy of a literal translation. If your pastor preaches from a particular version, you might want to choose that version as your daily translation. Most translations are now available with introductory notes on each book, commentary on difficult passages, and other reference material such as maps. And many translations are found online or on an app for your phone.

COMPARISON OF TRANSLATIONS BY METHOD

Literal ◄————►	Dynamic Equivalence ◄————►	Paraphrase
King James Version	New International Version	Living Bible
New King James Version	New Living Translation	The Message
English Standard Version	Good News Bible	Contemporary English Version
New American Standard	New Jerusalem Bible Version	
New Revised Standard Version		

Changing Languages

Translators must also contend with the reality that English, like all languages, is constantly changing. New translations must continually be produced so each new generation can understand what God is saying. Many Christians become attached to their favorite translation. Some go further and criticize other translations as unspiritual. Don't fall into this trap. Remember, each translation philosophy has value, and new translations are essential for allowing people to hear the Bible's message for themselves.

Which translation does your pastor use? Which type of translation seems most useful to you?

HOW THE BIBLE IS ARRANGED

At any public library or bookstore, you'll find a wide variety of books: fiction, nonfiction, juvenile, poetry, reference, and many more. When you visit the library or bookstore, it's helpful to know how the material is arranged so you can easily find what you're looking for. The Bible is like that. It's really a whole library or bookstore contained in a single volume. It contains sixty-six books in at least eight categories of literature.

Knowing the Layout

Thirty-nine books comprise the Old Testament; there are twenty-seven in the New Testament. Books of the Bible are divided into chapters and verses. The usual way of giving the address for a part of the Bible is to list the book, then the chapter number followed by a colon, then the verse number or numbers. For example, Matthew 4:1–11 means that the passage is in the book of Matthew, chapter 4, verses 1 through 11. You'll also see the names of the books abbreviated (for example, Matt. 4:1–11).

The first five books in the Bible are called the Pentateuch. They begin with the account of creation and tell the history of the Hebrews until they are about to enter the Promised Land.

Next come the Historical Books, which continue Jewish history from the entry into the Promised Land until about 400 BC. The next section turns away from history to present a poetic picture of life within Israel, the Poetical Books. The final section in the Old Testament contains the writings of the Prophets.

The New Testament picks up the story about four hundred years after the last events of the Old Testament. The first four books are known as the Gospels, telling the story of Jesus' life, death, and resurrection. The next book describes the church's early history. A collection of letters follows, written by the apostle Paul and other church leaders. The last book explains how Jesus will return to complete the work God began at creation.

Review the table of contents in your Bible and find each book. You'll notice that some are very long while others are very brief. Read a sample of several books to note the different flavor of each writer.

OLD TESTATMENT

Pentateuch	History	Poetry	Prophecy
Genesis	Joshua	Job	Isaiah
Exodus	Judges	Psalms	Jeremiah
Leviticus	Ruth	Proverbs	Lamentations
Numbers	1 and 2 Samuel	Ecclesiastes	Ezekiel
Deuteronomy	1 and 2 Kings	Song of Songs	Daniel
	1 and 2 Chronicles		Hosea
	Ezra		Joel
	Nehemiah		Amos
	Esther		Obadiah
			Jonah
			Micah
			Nahum
			Habakkuk
			Zephaniah
			Haggai
			Zechariah
			Malachi

NEW TESTATMENT

Gospels	Paul's Epistles (Letters)	General Epistles (Letters)	
Matthew	Romans	Hebrews	
Mark	1 and 2 Corinthians	James	
Luke	Galatians	1 and 2 Peter	
John	Ephesians	1, 2, and 3 John	
	Philippians	Jude	
History	Colossians		
Acts	1 and 2 Thessalonians	**Prophecy**	
	1 and 2 Timothy	Revelation	
	Titus		
	Philemon		

Which book of the Bible seems most interesting to you? Why?

Knowing the Plot

Reading the Bible can be confusing because there are so many names, people, and places mentioned. But there is a connection between them! As you find and follow that connection, your journey through the Bible's pages will be more enjoyable.

Here's the story in a nutshell: In the beginning, God created a perfect world, in which our first parents felt at ease with God, themselves, and the natural world. Then disaster struck! Human beings disobeyed God. This act, sin, changed the world from a place where people felt at home to a place of violence, loneliness, and guilt. What did God do about this? That is the story of the rest of the Bible.

God's first step was to choose an older couple, Abraham and Sarah. He called them to leave their homeland and become nomads. In return, he promised them a new homeland and many descendants. They had no children of their own, and Sarah was past childbearing age, but God gave them a son, Isaac. Through Isaac and his son Jacob, God brought many descendants, known first as Hebrews, then as Israelites, and finally as Jews.

God planned to use the Jews as key agents in his plan to save the world. The Old Testament tells how God made a family into a nation with its own laws, land, and leader. Unfortunately, they stumbled and disobeyed God. He had to discipline them, but he did not abandon them.

When the time was right, God sent his Son, Jesus, into the world. Jesus came as a Jewish baby, born to Mary, a virgin. He grew up and began to teach other Jews. He chose twelve men as his close associates, who were known as apostles. Although the Jewish people gladly heard Jesus' teaching, the leaders were jealous and arranged to have Jesus killed. Little did they know that God would use Jesus' execution as the decisive blow against sin. On the third day after Jesus' death,

God raised him to life, proving his power over sin. The good news of Jesus' death and resurrection spread among the Jews. Eventually, the message spread to the Gentiles and around much of the world.

While the cross was the decisive moment, it was not the end of the battle. God continues to undo the effects of sin on the world. Much of what God is doing, we cannot see clearly. We do know, however, that he wants to work through the church. The church is to model and proclaim the good news that sin no longer has the power to control and ruin us. We are to show that God's power is stronger and his kingdom is growing. God did not leave the final victory up to us, however. He promises to intervene once again, finally and forever. Jesus will return and finish the work God started long ago.

USE THE BIBLE IN YOUR LIFE

The Bible, like anything else, is most profitable when we use it for its intended purpose. So why did God give us this book? Although it can teach us how to live and be good parents or what will happen when Jesus returns, these are not the primary reasons God gave us the Bible. He gave us this Book so we could know him. Therefore, the most important question to ask is always, "What can I learn about God from this passage?"

Learn about God

You don't need to be a Bible scholar to ask this question, just keep your eyes open for four things:

1. What the inspired authors say about God. For example, the apostle John told us, "God is love" (1 John 4:8).

2. What God says about himself. For example, we know that God never changes. He tells us so in Malachi 3:6.

3. What God does. For example, we see from God's parting of the Red Sea that he is mighty and powerful.

4. What God doesn't do or say. God's name never appears in the book of Esther, yet we learn from it that he spared his people from a great tragedy. This shows us God can control circumstances without taking direct action.

Look for the characteristics of God that underlie his actions. Your goal is to know him, not merely what he has done. Also, compare what you learn about God in one passage with what you have learned about him elsewhere in the Bible. You would not want people to base their opinion of you on only one action. In the same way, God reveals his character a bit at a time. Only by looking at the complete picture can we understand him properly.

Memorize Scripture

Once you learn something about God, hold on to it. Memorize passages from the Bible so you can recall these truths when you need them most. When you are frightened, you can remember that God is always present, as we see in Jesus' promise in Matthew 28:20: "And surely I am with you always, to the very end of the age." When you feel overwhelmed by circumstances, you can remember that God is all-powerful, "For nothing will be impossible with God" (Luke 1:37 ESV).

Each chapter in this book features a key verse. Begin the habit of Bible memorization with these important verses.

Overcome Temptation

As you get to know God through his Word, you will find it easier to say no when you are tempted to disobey him. Not surprisingly, the Serpent tempted Eve to disobey God by confusing her about what God had said and what he was like (see Gen. 3:1–5). Nor is it a surprise that Jesus resisted Satan's temptation by quoting Old Testament verses that spoke about God's character (see Matt. 4:1–11).

As you learn God's Word, you'll gain strength to fight temptation.

Be Changed

The goal in knowing the Bible, of course, is to grow in relationship with God. God did not give us this Book so we could study for a final exam. He told us what he is like so we can know him and become like him.

The true test of our Bible knowledge, therefore, is not how well we recite facts, but how well we live. If we know that God is all-powerful, we will demonstrate that by trusting him and remaining at peace during difficult circumstances. As we come to understand that God is merciful, we will put that knowledge into action by accepting his mercy when we stumble and by showing mercy to others.

You have started on your personal journey of faith. To make the most of your trip, get to know the One who made this journey possible and who travels with you. He has revealed himself to you through the Bible, so read it, study it, and put it to use in your life.

If you allow it, God will use his Word to teach, train, and correct you as needed so that you'll become a godly person, "thoroughly equipped for every good work" (2 Tim. 3:17).

What role does the Bible play in your life? List some benefits that you gain from knowing God's Word.

LIVE TO WORSHIP IN EVERYTHING

Let everything that has breath praise the LORD.
Praise the LORD.
—Psalm 150:6

BIBLE BASICS

- Psalm 150:1–6

As you read the above passage, note the variety and intensity of ways in which we are told to worship God. How is your worship similar to this description? How is it different?

GOD FIRST

The struggle between human beings and God has always concerned the issue of control. That is, who is in charge of your life, you or God?

The first pages of the Bible reveal that Adam and Eve's original sin was committed precisely because of their desire to be in charge. When God said, "Don't," Adam and Eve said, "We will if we want to!"

Worship is the act of putting God first in your life. In this chapter, you will learn why worship is important for a Christian and how you can worship in daily life. As you learn to "bow the knee" to God and acknowledge his lordship over the world and yourself, your life will take on new meaning and you will discover the joy of exalting Christ.

CORPORATE WORSHIP

Throughout the history of God's people, there have been two general contexts for worship: public (corporate) and private (personal).

Examples of corporate worship fill the New Testament, occasions when people gathered to honor God through song, testimony, prayer, preaching, and teaching. The writer of one New Testament book challenged God's people to "not [give] up meeting together" (Heb. 10:25). This is God's way of telling you that your life will be enhanced by regularly gathering with like-minded followers of Christ.

First Corinthians 12 shows us that each part of Christ's "body" has value to the others. Corporate worship allows us to function as a body. It enables us to meet each other's needs to a greater degree than if each of us interacted with God only in private.

Activity

Corporate worship can be formal or informal. It may include a good deal of liturgy (structured participation by the congregation), or it may be laid-back and casual. Scripture does not prescribe the level of formality that should characterize a worship service. It does, however, suggest elements that should be included in corporate worship:

- Music (see Ps. 92:1; 96:1; Eph. 5:19)
- Prayer (see Acts 1:14; 2:42)
- An affirmation of faith (see 1 Cor. 15:3–5; for example, the Apostles' Creed)
- Personal testimonies (see 1 John 1:1–3)
- Giving tithes and offerings (see Deut. 16:17; Mal. 3:10; 1 Cor. 16:1–2)
- Baptism (see Acts 16:13–15)
- The Lord's Supper (see 1 Cor. 11:23–26)
- Scripture reading (see Luke 4:16–21)
- Preaching (see Acts 8:4; 15:35)

This list demonstrates the many ways in which a group might express its love and devotion to God and his kingdom. Each element contains its own potential for variety and intensity of expression.

Variety

There can be more than one method of expression for corporate worship. For example, tremendous variety in music characterizes worship in churches today. Some churches use instruments; others don't. Some only use an organ; others add a piano, guitar, or drums. And the type of music used in church may range from chants to hymns to choruses.

Variety may also be seen in the practice of prayer in various churches or even within the same congregation. Prayer may be offered silently, read aloud, or given extemporaneously.

Even the sacraments, baptism and Communion, may be observed in a variety of ways. Baptism may take the form of immersion, sprinkling, or pouring. And the Lord's Supper may be received while seated, standing, or kneeling.

There really are many ways to express praise and thanks to God. Every congregation probably has a favorite way of approaching God, but it's refreshing to try new things in corporate worship.

Intensity

We don't speak all our words with the same intensity. A rousing "Hurray!" shouted at a sporting event will be spoken with more energy than an "I love you" whispered to a loved one. Both are sincere expressions of emotion, but they vary in intensity.

In the same way, the intensity of corporate worship may vary according to the occasion. We may be quiet, reflective, jubilant, weepy, remorseful, or grateful at different times. Sometimes, a slow, moving musical piece may communicate the mood of our worship. Another time, the crash of a cymbal offered in praise to God might be more appropriate.

In the Bible, you will observe physical expressions of worship such as clapping, bowing, dancing, and lying prostrate before the Lord. Prayer, too, may vary in intensity, sometimes being offered quietly— even silently—and at other times being spoken with tears.

All of these expressions are acceptable and meaningful when done unto the Lord. It is important to note that God calls all of it a "joyful noise" (even if it's not exactly on key!).

TWO STYLES OF MODERN WORSHIP		
	Formal	**Informal**
Atmosphere	Often quiet, reflective	Often celebratory, "noisy"
Music	Primarily hymns	Primarily choruses
Prayers	May be written	Usually extemporaneous
Instruments	Organ and piano, primarily	Guitar, drums, electronic keyboard
Affirmation of Faith	By recitation of creeds	By personal testimony
Sermon	Delivered from a manuscript	Delivered from an outline or notes

Do you prefer a formal or informal style of corporate worship? Why?

PERSONAL WORSHIP

Personal worship is private worship—it's done solo, just you worshiping God. It's important for each of us to have daily time with God, encountering him in the midst of everyday living.

The New Testament shows that Jesus had private time with his heavenly Father, often early in the morning. In Psalm 5:3, David expressed a desire to meet with the Lord each morning to "lay [his] requests before [him] and wait expectantly." Genesis tells us that Adam, the first person in the world, walked with God each day, enjoying fellowship and closeness with his Creator.

Find some quiet time each day to spend alone with God, talking, singing, listening, weeping, or rejoicing. It may last an hour or only fifteen minutes. Length is not as important as depth. The purpose is to connect with God through worship—to know him better and to love him more deeply.

Scripture gives little detail on how to fill this daily time with God. Therefore, a variety of activities have been developed to aid in this encounter of God. Certainly, Bible reading and prayer will be essential. Here are two options for your personal prayer time.

The ACTS Method

One method suggests the use of four elements in daily prayer that form the acronym ACTS.

- A—Adoration. Begin your prayer time by expressing worship and love to God and Christ.
- C—Confession. Allow the Spirit to explore your weakness and sinfulness. Confess your sin to God and receive his forgiveness.
- T—Thanksgiving. Give thanks to God for his goodness to you.
- S—Supplication. Ask God for his help. Share your requests with him and let him know you trust him to meet your needs.

The Lord's Prayer

Another simple plan for daily prayer uses the Lord's Prayer as a guide (see Matt. 6:9–13). Jesus' foundational prayer included statements on these elements:

- Adoration: "Our Father in heaven, hallowed be your name."
- Subjection: "Your will be done on earth."
- Requests: "Give us today our daily bread."
- Confession: "Forgive us our debts."
- Reconciliation: "As we also have forgiven our debtors."

- Strength: "Lead us not into temptation."
- Protection: "Deliver us from the evil one."

Remember, there is no single correct formula for moving closer to God. In fact, it is good to sometimes just be silent before the Lord. To realize one's daily dependence upon God can be a most empowering experience.

What are the benefits of having a daily time with God? List some things that can interfere with you having this regular time with God.

THE THEOLOGY OF WORSHIP

The biblical words for worship refer to the act of bowing down, or prostrating oneself, before a more worthy person. The basis of our worship is our belief that Jesus Christ is Lord and that God's will is to be desired and obeyed.

When you read the Bible, you will find that worshiping God has always been a central activity for his followers. The book of Revelation contains many references to worshiping God in heaven (for example, Rev. 5:8–9; 11:16–18; 14:3; 15:3–4). In the Old Testament temple, the people offered sacrifices of worship to God at various times throughout the year. When Mary, mother of Jesus, found out that she was pregnant with God's Son, she cried out in a song of worship (see Luke 1:46–55). The book of Acts describes the early church's passion for worship (see Acts 2:42–47; 16:25).

Beginning with the time of Moses, we can see four distinct periods in the life of God's people, each with its own style of worship.

Time Period	Place of Worship
Wilderness wanderings	A moveable tabernacle
Occupying the Promised Land	A permanent temple
The scattering of the Jews throughout the world	A local synagogue
The early Christian church	House churches

Places of Worship

First is the Old Testament period of the tabernacle. The tabernacle was a meeting tent that the Israelites used for worship as they traveled throughout the desert.

The second period began when the Israelites built a permanent worship structure called the temple. Here, the worship experience became highly structured.

The third period was defined by the use of the synagogue. The Jews who lived in exile developed this institution. Synagogues were constructed wherever Jews lived. Synagogue activity was based on instruction more than on worship.

Fourth is the New Testament period of the house church. Early Christians gathered to worship, typically in someone's home.

Our modern period began when Christianity was recognized as a legal religion in the fourth century. During this time, the first buildings for Christian worship were erected. Worship became very ritualized, using symbols and the written word to guide the worshiper.

The Meaning of Worship

Our word *worship* is derived from the old English term *worth-ship*. To worship really means to ascribe worth or value to someone or something.

Three questions to assist the worshiper in determining the worth of who is worshiped are:

- What value do you place on this act?
- Do the praises of the worshipers indicate their awareness of the traits of the object of their worship?
- Does the worship come from the heart?

Theology is never meant to be a "stand-alone" pursuit. It is not an end in itself. A theology of worship, therefore, should lead us to a deeper appreciation of the One being worshiped.

First Chronicles 16:25 states, "Great is the LORD and *most worthy of praise*" (emphasis added). Jesus told his followers that whoever wishes to be a worshiper must "worship in the *Spirit* and in *truth*" (John 4:24, emphasis added). His statement implies an integration of theology and feeling, intellect and heart. The biblical stories of how people worshiped "back then" were written to inspire our worship today.

THE PURPOSE OF WORSHIP

Why is it so important that we worship God? What is the point of our worship? Our worship has at least five purposes that will produce results in our lives and relationship with God.

To Ascribe

The first purpose is to ascribe worthiness to God. He alone desires our worship and affection. His position as Creator of all things gives him the right to be worshiped.

To Align

Worship's second purpose is to align us with the will of God. Jeremiah 29:11 states that God has a plan for each person's life. Through worship we surrender our will for ourselves and submit to his will for us.

To Acknowledge

To remind us of and allow us to acknowledge our total dependence upon God is the third purpose of worship. Until we realize our total dependence upon God—for this life and for eternal life—we will never fully attain the "abundant life" that Jesus promised. Scripture tells us that God inhabits the praises of his people (see Ps. 22:3 KJV). When we worship God, we invite him into our daily lives. Proverbs 3:6 promises that if we are willing to acknowledge him, "he will make [our] paths straight." Worshiping God affects the direction of our lives.

To Admit

The fourth purpose is to be a means for us to recognize and admit our sinfulness and our need for forgiveness. The Bible tells us that we all "fall short" (Rom. 3:23), that we are "dead in [our] sins" (Eph. 2:1), and that we need to be "born again" (John 3:3). When we confess our sins to God, he faithfully and lovingly forgives us and cleanses us from guilt (see 1 John 1:9). That is accomplished through worship. In our worship, we can admit our need for forgiveness and receive God's pardon.

To Admire

Fifth, we worship to admire God's constant involvement in our lives. We don't need to look far to see God's fingerprints on our lives. He has been good to us, and he has protected us. He has given us wisdom when called for, and he has generously given us everything we have needed to enjoy this life. In other words, he has lovingly protected us as his precious children. The act of worship allows us to thank our heavenly Father who has so richly blessed us.

God created human beings to worship. That is why we often run wildly in pursuit of other things and other people. We are trying to satisfy our need to ascribe value to something or someone other than ourselves. Jesus acknowledged this tendency in Matthew 6:33, where he lovingly told his followers to seek God's kingdom *first*.

Which of the five purposes for worship comes most naturally to you? With which ones do you struggle? Why?

THE ACT OF WORSHIP

In the dictionary, *worship* is listed first as a noun. But worship is primarily a verb—it's something we do! It is an action of the heart. It is the primary act for which God created us.

In the garden of Eden, our first parents chose to take their own path. They chose to take their way instead of God's. Ever since that fateful moment, the human heart has been restless. The act of worship is the secret to our contentment. "Bowing the knee" before almighty God is a wonderfully freeing act. This is the irony of worship. To submit oneself to God is to live in true freedom.

We *do* worship. Our hearts ascribe worth or value to something or someone. When we choose to worship God, our outward actions expose the inner posture of our hearts. The symbols of worship (lifting hands, kneeling, quietness, singing, etc.) all express our deep passion, submission, and gratitude to a generous and awesome God.

COMMIT TO
THE FELLOWSHIP

From him the whole body, joined and held together
by every supporting ligament, grows and builds
itself up in love, as each part does its work.

—Ephesians 4:16

BIBLE BASICS

- Ephesians 4:2–6, 11–16

Where do you see yourself contributing to the life of your church?

GOD'S TEAM

Everyone loves to be on a team, especially a winning team, but
we all know a team is stronger than any of its individual members.
That strength comes from shared goals, a common vision, and the joy
of working together to win. Close relationships develop through the

ups and downs — the victories and setbacks — of team life. A dynamic, an X-factor, develops within a team, which cannot be easily explained. It must be experienced to be understood.

The family of faith is a team. We function together more powerfully than any one of us can alone. The body of Christ has a dynamic like the X-factor of a winning team, but we must experience it to appreciate it.

Let's look at some of the components that create this dynamic, this fellowship, in the family of God. These components are part of what makes a team of believers uniquely powerful together. Here's what it's like to be on God's team.

BAPTISM

Every team has its own rituals and traditions. Baseball teams are notoriously superstitious. Many baseball players, for instance, avoid stepping on the chalk lines of the field. Football teams have their own rituals, such as the coin toss at the start of the game and the pep talk at halftime. A team gains identity and solidarity from its traditions.

The family of God has traditions, too. The most important of these are called sacraments, rituals that Jesus instituted to bring us closer to God. More powerful than mere human traditions, these sacred rites are actually a means of grace. When we participate in them, we communicate with God in a special way.

The first of these is baptism.

Jesus himself was baptized with water (see Matt. 3:13–16), and he commanded his disciples to baptize others as they went into the world with the gospel story (see Matt. 28:16–20). His baptism launched his public ministry, and his final instructions to the disciples included the command to baptize. Why was this "dip in the brook" so important? Why should I be baptized?

Reasons to Be Baptized

Here are a few reasons why baptism has been significant to Christians from New Testament times until now.

It's a Public Statement of Faith. By the act of baptism, the baptized person declares to the world that he or she is a Christian. That's why baptism for new believers is often held outdoors in a public place. It provides a clear way to announce that the baptized believer has joined the team! Even if baptism is held in a church or semiprivate setting, the message is the same. It declares to all present that the individual has chosen to follow Christ.

It's a Statement of Accountability. When baptized we are asked to declare our intention to live for Christ. An affirmative response puts us "on the record" as being serious about following Christ. We make a statement to our teammates, our brothers and sisters in Christ, that we aim to lead a new life.

It's a Symbol of Salvation. Baptism is a graphic reminder of what happened in us when we were saved. When we pledged our faith in Christ, his blood washed away our sins and made us part of his family. It is as if the person we used to be died, just as Christ died on the cross, and was raised to a new life. Baptism illustrates the cleansing of our lives by "washing with water." It also illustrates our death and resurrection with Christ (see Rom. 6:1–4). Baptism does not literally wash away our sins; it merely illustrates what God has done in our hearts.

It's a Statement of Unity. Baptism is a celebration, like the victory lap after a race or a homecoming parade for an Olympic champion. It builds the Christian team's morale to realize that others have joined the family of faith and are taking a public stand for Christ.

Have you been baptized? List reasons you would consider being baptized.

Ways to Be Baptized

The methods of baptism have been the subject of strong discussion throughout church history. There are three basic methods that are used.

Immersion. The candidate for baptism is totally immersed in water. Immersion may be performed outdoors in a river, lake, or other body of water, or indoors in a baptismal tank. Many prefer this because it graphically depicts our death and resurrection with Christ.

Pouring. Water is poured over the person's head and flows down over much of the body. This is frequently used where access to open water is not available or is felt unnecessary. It provides a visual reminder that Christ's blood has washed away sin.

Sprinkling. A small amount of water is sprinkled on the candidate's head. This method is typically used for infant baptism and for those who are physically unable to be baptized by immersion or pouring. Some churches simply prefer this and view it as symbolic of our cleansing by the blood of Christ.

Who Should Be Baptized

While there may be some disagreements concerning the preferred method of baptism, there is unanimous agreement that all believers should be baptized. "Believer's baptism" is the term for the baptism of adults who have professed their faith in Christ.

Many churches also baptize infants. Why would we do that, since an infant cannot make a decision to accept Christ as Savior?

We may baptize infants because we believe that God's grace extends to all people who are not able to choose right from wrong. The Bible teaches that those who are too young to understand the truth are not responsible for the truth (see Mark 10:13–16; Acts 2:38–39). When a person reaches the "age of accountability"—in other words, an age when he or she is old enough to understand the difference between right and wrong and respond to the gospel—that person becomes accountable to God. Prior to that time, they are under the protection of God's grace. This is called the prevenient grace of God—the grace that "goes before." Parents may choose to have their infants baptized as an acknowledgment of God's grace and of their own faith in Christ.

Every believer should be baptized!

What questions do you have about baptism and whether or not you should be baptized?

THE LORD'S SUPPER

The Lord's Supper. Communion. The Eucharist. Commemoration of the Last Supper. Breaking of bread.

All of these terms refer to the same observance in church life. When Christ was facing the last hours before the crucifixion, he instructed his disciples to prepare a special meal (see Matt. 26:26–29; Luke 22:14–20). At that meal, Jesus instituted the church's second sacrament, the Lord's Supper. Today, we observe this ritual as a reminder of Christ's death and as a means of growing closer to God.

Old Testament Roots

Since the days when God miraculously delivered the Israelites from slavery in Egypt, Jewish people have observed the Passover Feast. This feast commemorates the crucial event that moved the Egyptian king to release the Hebrew people from slavery (see Ex. 11–12).

On that fateful night, the angel of death moved through the land and killed the firstborn son in every home. But houses with blood sprinkled on the doorposts were spared. These houses were "passed over."

On the night before he was crucified, Christ ate the Passover meal with his disciples. He told them of a new and far greater salvation that God was bringing to the world. This deliverance from captivity would no longer be remembered as "then and there" but would be experienced "here and now." He was speaking of his death, which brought deliverance from sin.

Passover: The Old Covenant	The Lord's Supper: The New Covenant
Commemorates deliverance from slavery in Egypt	Recalls our deliverance from sin
Applies only to Jewish people	Is for all who believe in Christ
Is a memory of past glory	Is a celebration of present reality

Remembering Christ's Death

When Christ talked with his disciples that night, he told them to remember this new arrangement, the new covenant, that God was making with them (see Luke 22:20). Paul the apostle restated that instruction to the church at Corinth (1 Cor. 11:23–26). When we observe the Lord's Supper, we are following Jesus' command to remember the salvation that he provided for us. This act brings us into close fellowship, or communion, with God.

In his instructions about the Lord's Supper, Paul warned against receiving this sacrament in an "unworthy manner" and made it clear that the Lord's Supper is exclusively for members of the Lord's family (1 Cor. 11:27–30). A person should be in a right standing with God when he or she participates in the Lord's Supper.

Here are important points to remember about the Lord's Supper:

- It is a time to remember the death of Christ and to be thankful for the sacrifice he made.
- It is a time for self-examination and for seeking forgiveness for things in our lives that displease him.
- It is to be observed periodically by Christians meeting together.
- It is for believers only, since those who do not know Christ do not understand the true meaning of the Lord's Supper.

Communion is a time to celebrate our unity as a team and remember our Lord's sacrifice.

Have you observed the Lord's Supper since you became a Christian? Describe your experience and how you felt as you joined in.

THE CHURCH

If you work for a large corporation, you might have coworkers who live in various parts of the country, even in various parts of the world. Although you have separate workplaces, you still share the same corporate goals and objectives. You are all part of the same team.

The church of Jesus Christ is like that. Millions of Christians live in many countries around the world and worship in churches with different names, yet we are all one family—one team.

One Tree, Many Branches

For more than a thousand years after Christ lived here on earth, the church more or less functioned as a single unit. There were no denominations as we now know them. Most of those who called themselves Christian were part of one church, whose earthly leader was located in Rome.

Over time, however, certain incorrect ideas became common, and various practices developed that concerned many people.

One of those concerned persons was a German monk named Martin Luther, who lived in the sixteenth century. In 1517 he nailed a ninety-five-point document—his list of protests against the church—to a church door in the town of Wittenberg. He hoped to stir debate over a number of issues that troubled him. Initially, not much happened. Within a few months, however, reaction to Luther's document grew quite strong. Over time, those who agreed with his protests came to be known as Protestants. Some people formed churches separate from the Roman church.

In the next 250 years or so—until about 1800—many of the oldest denominations in the Protestant family came into being. Reformers like Luther formed some. Revivalists like John Wesley, the eighteenth-century English clergyman who started the Methodist movement, began others. Since then, new Christian denominations have come into existence occasionally by revival or reform movements.

Today, there are many denominations as Christians have gathered themselves into the groups they believe best represent Christ's teachings.

All strive to faithfully follow the teachings of Jesus but operate independently of one another.

What do you think are the key beliefs that make a church part of the Christian family?

Teamwork

Every member of a team is responsible to the others. In hockey, for instance, teamwork is evident in every game. Veteran players set an example for the rookie players. If a member of the opposing team roughs up the goaltender, teammates come to defend their goalie. When the coach gives instruction, all the players follow the direction, whether they are rookies or veterans.

Team responsibilities exist in the family of faith just as they do in sports. We have lateral responsibilities—responsibilities to other members of our team. This is called interdependence. We have vertical responsibilities—responsibilities to those over us in the faith, such as pastors. This is called accountability. We have nurturing responsibilities for those who are younger in the faith. This is called mentoring. We have a responsibility to all members of the family of faith to live faithfully. This is Christian citizenship. At the apex of it all, we have responsibility to, and will give an account to, the head coach—Christ.

Relationship within the Body	Scripture
Interdependence	Galatians 6:1–2
Accountability	Romans 3:19
Mentoring	1 Kings 19:19–21; 2 Kings 2:1–18
Christian Citizenship	Romans 12:9–21
Ultimate Accountability	Romans 14:12

Describe your relationship with other believers—for example, those at your local church, your pastor, and Christians in other denominations.

JOINING THE TEAM

As individuals, most of us like the idea of being in charge, being independent, and living by our own rules. As members of Christ's body, however, we are accountable to God. We are dependent on him for life itself and are interdependent with our brothers and sisters in the faith. We need one another for love, support, and understanding; and we submit ourselves to Christ's authority. That's quite an adjustment! But in God's family, what we give up is of lesser value than what we receive. That's the value of the team.

We Need Each Other

Every Christian needs to be connected with a local unit of the body of Christ. There have always been religious hermits who lock themselves away from the world in a vain attempt to keep sin at bay. However, isolationists rob themselves of the value of team camaraderie. The thundering call from two thousand years of Christian history is that we really do need each other (see Heb. 10:25).

Paul wrote two letters to a young church in the city of Corinth. In one of these letters, he spoke at length about the need for all believers to pool together their various gifts and talents so the body of Christ might be healthy and growing. He likened the church to a human body that has various parts, each necessary for the body to function properly (1 Cor. 12:12–31). The church needs us, and we need the church!

We must interact with the body of Christ to become strong and healthy believers. There are a few exceptions, of course. Some Christians thrive in spirit while cut off from the rest of the body of Christ due to imprisonment, extended illness, geographic isolation, or some other circumstance. God's grace is adequate in such cases.

But in our normal life cycle, isolation produces spiritually stunted people with a very limited worldview and little to no opportunity to exercise their spiritual gifts for the common good. The wholesome interaction of relationships within the body fosters maturity and allows for the exercise of gifts and talents. It helps create the strength that comes only from standing together.

Maximum Impact

Let's recall the example of a sports team. One player, no matter how skilled, gifted, and determined he may be, is no match for an opposing team. He can never win a game single-handedly. So it is with us. No matter how gifted we may be, alone we are just that—alone— and have only the power of one. Joined with other believers in a healthy body, we greatly expand our impact for God and good.

In Leviticus 26:8, we find this incredible truth: "Five of you will chase a hundred, and a hundred of you will chase ten thousand, and your enemies will fall by the sword before you."

Do the math. Five with God took on 100—a ratio of 1 to 20. One hundred with God took on 10,000—a ratio of 1 to 100. The number of "good guys" went up from 5 to 100. The number of "bad guys" went up from 100 to 10,000, but still victory was assured.

Together we are stronger.

This is called synergy: maximized output that results from working together. Synergy exists in the body of Christ. Isolation fosters desolation; partnerships foster power. Independence fosters loneliness; community fosters strength.

In what ways are you connecting in your church? Which Sunday school class, small group, or discipleship group have you joined?

The Church Universal and the Local Church

The church universal—all true believers in Jesus Christ—is an awesome array of people from every point in history and every conceivable racial, geographic, cultural, and language group. When assembled together, as the Bible promises will occur in the last days (see Rev. 7:9–17), the church universal will be an incredible gathering, the magnitude and scope of which we can only imagine. We, too, will be a part of that incredible gathering as we remain true to Christ as Savior. That grand assembly will be the church in its most expansive and exciting reality.

The church in our time has many valid expressions around the world. In other words, there is one true church, yet there may be many local churches. Practices and customs may vary from one congregation to the next. Churches may exist under a variety of names. Positions on issues of lesser importance may differ. There are many ways of worshiping together, and some Christians will staunchly defend their way of "doing church." But that's like bickering with your brother or sister over who should have the TV remote control. We are still family, even when we feud over how that family will function.

The true church is one, and we are all part of that family through faith in Jesus Christ. We have accepted him as Savior. That's the basis of family living. We may disagree over the details of family life, but we all belong.

These various expressions of church life actually give us strength as a body. Different approaches to these matters may appeal to different individuals. If all churches were exactly the same, how boring and limited we would be! Our varied approaches to church life allow people to seek and find a church home that is an authentic part of the body of Christ, yet suits their own needs.

Remember, though, that not all groups who use the word *church* to define themselves accept the clear teaching of the Bible on matters of salvation and other vital issues. When seeking fellowship with other believers, we must be careful to associate with those who are, in truth, members of the family of faith.

Finding a Local Church

After accepting Christ as Savior, one of the most crucial questions you must answer is: Where will I make my church home? This will be where you will invest your life for the kingdom, use your gifts in ministry, and receive teaching and encouragement in the faith. This is no small decision.

Christians sometimes select a local church based on good but secondary factors, such as:

- Proximity to home
- Association with family
- Appearance of facilities
- Quality of music
- Personality of the pastor

While these factors may initially attract you to a particular congregation, you need to consider some other, more important issues. Here are some questions you might ask when choosing a local church:

- Does this church accurately teach the truth of Scripture?
- Are people coming to Christ through the ministries of the church?
- Will I have a place of meaningful ministry in this church?
- Do I sense the presence of the Holy Spirit when I worship there?
- Do the sermons help me understand the faith and help me cope with everyday life?
- Do the people have a unified passion to build the kingdom?

If the answers to these questions are all positive, you might consider secondary factors such as the music, facilities, and church programs. If the answers to these questions were "yes," then it's likely that the secondary factors will be positive also.

Here are some other questions you might ask as you look for a local church:

- What is the church's statement of faith? Does it fit with what I know about the Bible?
- What are the mission, vision, and core values of the church? Does the congregation seem to have a clear idea of why it exists and what it is doing?
- What is the congregation's position on important social issues such as abortion, homosexuality, pornography, and euthanasia?
- What am I looking for in a church? Do I want to serve others, or do I want to be served?

A healthy local church is the essence of the body of Christ. The apostle Paul drew a parallel between the relationship that exists in a healthy marriage and the relationship that exists between Christ and the church. He said that Christ loves the church and gave his life for it (Eph. 5:22–33). Jesus said that he would build the church and that even hell cannot stop it (Matt. 16:13–18)!

So the church really is important. And as a new believer, you will need to become a part of it. Select a congregation carefully, commit to it fully, and participate in it gladly. There are no perfect churches, so seek fellowship, not perfection, in a church. You will discover the great joy of life in a healthy local church.

What are some preferences that affect your choice of a church? Which ones are negotiable? Which ones will you not compromise?

Joining a Church

Perhaps you have already found a healthy local church to call home. Since you have already decided to make this your church home, in one sense you have already joined the group. Membership in the church universal is based only on your faith in Christ. When you accepted him as your Savior, you "joined" the church.

Yet you should consider formalizing your relationship with a local congregation by becoming a member of that church. Why?

Let's return to the sports team analogy. When you join a team, you receive a uniform. You wear the colors of your team. That identifies you as one of the group, fosters loyalty to the team, and, as a practical matter, makes it easier to play the game.

When you join a local church, you become part of that local team. Here are some good reasons for doing that:

- It makes clear that you agree with that local church's mission and vision.
- It places you in an accountability relationship with other members of that church.

- It lets the other members know they can count on you for support.
- It may make you eligible for ministry or leadership responsibilities.

When you join a church, you come off the sidelines and get into the game. You become a fully functioning member of the team. Being a part of a healthy local church is a great and worthwhile experience. Go ahead; put on the colors!

Privileges of Membership	Responsibilities of Membership
Fellowship with other believers	Support of others by prayer, presence, ministry, and finances
Input on direction and vision for future	Support of the church's mission
Protection and support of the body	Promote the ministry of the church
Opportunities for leadership	Live a life that is a positive witness to the faith
Selection of pastoral leadership as needed	Serve in leadership roles as selected
"Wear the colors"—Be part of the team!	"Wear the colors"—Be part of the team!

Can a person be a Christian and not join a church? Why or why not?

EMBRACE THE MYSTERY OF THE TRIUNE GOD

Therefore go and make disciples of all nations, baptizing them in the name of the Father and of the Son and of the Holy Spirit.

—Matthew 28:19

BIBLE BASICS

- Matthew 3:13–17
- Matthew 28:18–20
- 2 Corinthians 13:14

Circle the references to the Father, Son, and Holy Spirit in each of the three passages. What do these references tell you about God?

ONE AND THREE

God is one — and yet three persons! This teaching is called the doctrine of the Trinity. It means that God is three persons, while at the same time, he is one.

How did Christians arrive at this concept of God? How did this doctrine develop in the early church? This belief is clearly found in the both the New Testament and the Old Testament and was the firmly held belief of the earliest Christians.

THE WITNESS OF THE NEW TESTAMENT

First, let's look at what the New Testament says about the Trinity.

Evidence for the Oneness of God

Jesus made clear the oneness of God in his High Priestly Prayer for his disciples the night before the crucifixion. He said to the Father, "Now this is eternal life: that they know you, the only true God, and Jesus Christ, whom you have sent" (John 17:3). Paul also repeatedly emphasized the oneness: "Yet for us there is but one God, the Father, from whom all things came and for whom we live; and there is but one Lord, Jesus Christ, through whom all things came and through whom we live" (1 Cor. 8:6). "There is one body and one Spirit, just as you were called to one hope when you were called; one Lord, one faith, one baptism; one God and Father of all, who is over all and through all and in all" (Eph. 4:4–6).

Evidence for the Threeness of God

The New Testament also reveals the threeness of God. The first of our key passages, Matthew 3:13–17, relates Jesus' baptism, the public act that marked the beginning of his public ministry. As Jesus came up out of the water, heaven opened and the Spirit of God descended like a dove and settled on him. And the Father spoke from heaven saying, "This is my Son, whom I love; with him I am well pleased" (3:17). All three persons of the Trinity were present.

The second key passage, Matthew 28:18–20, contains the Great Commission that Jesus gave to his disciples. He commanded them to "go and make disciples of all nations, baptizing them in the name of the Father and of the Son and of the Holy Spirit."

The third key passage, 2 Corinthians 13:14, gives the benediction with which Paul closed his second letter to the Corinthians. The church has used this benediction ever since Paul's day: "May the grace of the Lord Jesus Christ, and the love of God, and the fellowship of the Holy Spirit be with you all."

Many other New Testament passages could be cited. One is Peter's greeting in his first letter. He addressed those "who have been chosen according to the foreknowledge of God the Father, through the sanctifying work of the Spirit, to be obedient to Jesus Christ and sprinkled with his blood" (1 Pet. 1:2).

Evidence That Jesus Is God

The New Testament further emphasizes the threeness of God by the fact that both the Father and Jesus are called God. In Matthew 1:23, the angel told Joseph that the child to be born will be called "Immanuel (which means, 'God with us')." In John 1:1–3, we read, "In the beginning was the Word, and the Word was with God, and the Word was

God. He was with God in the beginning. Through him all things were made; without him nothing was made that has been made." John made it clear in the following verse that he was writing about Jesus, affirming in John 1:18, "No one has ever seen God, but the one and only Son, who is himself God and is in closest relationship with the Father, has made him known." In Romans 9:5, Paul identified Jesus as "the Messiah, who is God over all." In Titus 2:13, Paul wrote that we are awaiting "the appearing of the glory of our great God and Savior, Jesus Christ." And in Peter's introduction to his second letter, he addressed "those who through the righteousness of our God and Savior Jesus Christ have received a faith as precious as ours" (2 Pet. 1:1).

Evidence That the Holy Spirit Is God

The Scriptures make clear that the Holy Spirit is also God. He receives equal prominence as the other two persons of the Trinity at Jesus' baptism, in the baptismal formula, and in Paul's benediction. Even more significantly, three times in the New Testament a reference is made to the Holy Spirit, citing an Old Testament passage that refers to the one God, Yahweh, or Jehovah (LORD).

COMPARE THESE OLD TESTAMENT AND NEW TESTAMENT PASSAGES

Old Testament	New Testament	Comparison
Isaiah 6:5–10	Acts 28:25–27	
Exodus 17:7	Hebrews 3:7–9	
Jeremiah 31:31–34	Hebrews 10:15–17	

How do the Scriptures cited help you to understand the idea of God as Three-in-One?

THE WITNESS OF THE OLD TESTAMENT

We looked at the New Testament first because its testimony to God's threeness and oneness is quite clear and explicit. From that perspective, we now look at the Old Testament. While the Old Testament does not make such open and explicit references to the Trinity, many passages imply a plurality within God's singleness.

Evidence for the Oneness of God

The great passage on God's oneness is Deuteronomy 6:4: "Hear, O Israel: The LORD our God, the LORD is one." This verse is part of Israel's *Shema*, the confession of faith devout Jews recite every morning and evening.

Evidence for the Threeness of God

Possible references to God's threeness occur as early as Genesis 1. Genesis 1:1 uses the Hebrew name Elohim to identify the God who created. This word is a plural form and could be translated "gods." It was used in its plural form to refer to the Hebrews' God, also known by the Hebrew *Yahweh* or *Jehovah*. Hebrew grammarians explained that the word *Elohim* is a "plural of majesty, a plural of powers, or an intensive plural." But the possibility that the plural form implies more is heightened by other considerations in Genesis 1. The New Testament often uses "God" to refer specifically to the Father. And if we think of the Father as the Creator in Genesis 1:1, we find also that "the Spirit of God was hovering over the waters" (1:2), and that it was the spoken Word that brought light (and every other thing) into existence (1:3). John identified Jesus as the Word in the opening verses of his gospel.

We find another hint of God's threeness in Genesis 1:26 when Elohim ("God" in plural form) says, "Let *us* make mankind in *our* image, in *our* likeness." After Adam's fall in Eden, "the LORD God said, 'The man has now become like one of *us,* knowing good and evil' " (Gen. 3:22). And when Noah's descendants were building the tower of Babel, the Lord said, "Come, let *us* go down and confuse their language" (Gen. 11:7, emphasis added in all three quotations).

Isaiah contains strong implications of God's threeness. During Isaiah's transforming vision in the temple in Isaiah 6, he quotes the Lord as saying, "Whom shall *I* send? And who will go for *us*?" (6:8, emphasis added). In this context, the threefold cry of the seraphs may well provide a hint of praise to the three persons of the Trinity: "Holy, holy, holy is the LORD Almighty" (6:3). In Isaiah 61:1, the coming Messiah declared, "The Spirit of the Sovereign LORD is on me, because the LORD has anointed me." Here we may have the Father as the Sovereign Lord and the Holy Spirit as the Spirit of the Sovereign Lord. The "me" in this prophecy is the Son. Jesus made that clear when he read this passage in the synagogue at Nazareth and claimed to be its fulfillment (see Luke 4:16–21).

References to Christ

In addition to all of these, there are also several probable references to Christ in the Old Testament, particularly those to the "angel of the LORD," the "angel of God," and the "messenger of the covenant." The "angel of the LORD" appeared to Moses in the burning bush (Ex. 3:2), yet the one who spoke to Moses is sometimes also called "LORD" and "God." It is clear in Malachi 3:1 that the "messenger [same Hebrew word as *angel*] of the covenant" and the "Lord" are one and the same and that both refer to Christ.

References to the Holy Spirit

The Old Testament mentions the Spirit many times as the "Spirit of the LORD," the "Spirit of God" and even as the "Holy Spirit" (see Judg. 14:6, 19; 15:14; 1 Sam. 11:6; Isa. 63:10–11).

How do these Scriptures from the Old Testament strengthen for you the evidence for God as the three-in-one?

THE WITNESS OF THE EARLY CHURCH

What we have observed so far is very interesting. The Scriptures declare that God is one, yet they allude to his threeness, implicitly in the Old Testament and explicitly in the New Testament. But there is no systematic attempt to explain how God can be one and three at the same time.

You may have noticed that in our study of the Scriptures, we have not found any direct mention of the words *Trinity* or *persons*. Yet we use these terms. How did the early church move from the biblical statements to more formal doctrinal statements?

Development of Doctrines

The creeds and other doctrinal statements were not imposed on the church out of the blue by abstract theologians. Virtually every doctrine that was eventually accepted as orthodox (correct doctrine as recognized by the church) developed because some thinker proposed an interpretation of Scripture that the majority did not believe to be correct. In other words, the teaching of heresy (doctrine that differs from that generally accepted by the church) unwittingly benefited the church by clarifying the search for the truth.

Early Creeds and Doctrinal Statements

Even during the first century, while the New Testament was being written, the church was developing short, simple doctrinal statements, most of them dealing with who Jesus was. (Possible examples are 1 Cor. 15:3–4; Eph. 4:4–6; Phil. 2:5–11; Col. 1:13–20; 1 Tim. 3:l6— this last one is thought by some Bible scholars to be a hymn.) It is obvious that even then there were false teachers. Both Paul and John attempted to answer those who taught errors about Jesus. Some said Jesus was not God, while others said he was not a man, only a spirit who *appeared* to be a man.

One of the earliest Christian statements of belief appeared in Rome in the second century. It is referred to as the Old Roman Creed. In a somewhat later form, we know and repeat it as the Apostles' Creed— although the apostles did not write it:

I believe in God the Father Almighty, maker of heaven and earth;

And in Jesus Christ, his only Son, our Lord: who was con-ceived by the Holy Spirit, born of the Virgin Mary, suffered under Pontius Pilate, was crucified, dead, and buried; he descended into hell. The third day he rose again from the dead; he ascended into heaven, and sits at the right hand of God the Father Almighty; from there he shall come to judge the living and the dead.

I believe in the Holy Spirit, the holy catholic [or universal] church, the communion of saints, the forgiveness of sins, the resurrection of the body, and the life everlasting. Amen.

The Apostle's Creed, essentially an elaboration of the baptismal formula in Matthew 28:19, structures around the three persons of the

Trinity, focuses most of its contents on Jesus Christ, and touches on a few other matters after the reference to the Holy Spirit.

Three Basic Errors

While the New Testament did not explain how God was one and three simultaneously, the attempts of human teachers to reconcile this evidence forced the church to decide what was in harmony with the Scriptures and what was not. Three basic errors were expressed in those theories that were eventually condemned as heresies. The first error taught that there was only one indivisible God who showed himself at different times in three different ways—as the Father (the God of the Old Testament), the Son (Jesus in the New Testament), and the Holy Spirit (who was in the church and individual believers). The second error subordinated the Son and the Spirit to the Father in such a way that only the Father was truly God. And the third error so emphasized the threeness of God that it seemed to say there was not one God but three.

Formulation of the Nicene Creed

The church handled these challenges largely through councils of church leaders called bishops. One met at Nicea in AD 325, and expanded the Apostles' Creed into a Nicene Creed. It tackled the issue of the full deity of the Son and concluded by adding more explanation to the statement about Jesus Christ. He is "begotten of his Father before all worlds; God of God, Light of Light, very God of very God; begotten, not made, being of one substance with the Father, by whom all things were made." The church affirmed that anything less fell short of what the Bible revealed about Jesus.

Following this council, some teachers began to say that there was a "twoness" about God. They claimed the Father and the Son were both divine, but the Holy Spirit was not. Another council met at Constantinople in AD 381 to deal with this faulty doctrine. It expanded the creed by saying that the Holy Spirit is "the Lord and Giver of Life, who proceeds from the Father and the Son, who with the Father and Son together is worshiped and glorified; who spoke by the prophets." Again the church was convinced that anything less fell short of what the Bible revealed about the Holy Spirit.

If you had been present at the church councils, would you have agreed with the decisions? Why or why not?

THE MYSTERY OF THE TRINITY

It is obvious that the Scriptures made statements that forced the early church to deal theologically with the nature of God as both one and three. But our minds still struggle with what seem to be mutually exclusive concepts. Why is it so hard for us to understand the Trinity?

Limitations of the Human Mind

The problem is that the human mind cannot possibly comprehend God. We can recognize his existence, see his handiwork, sense his presence, and experience his mercy and grace. But we cannot fully understand him. We would have to be equal to him to understand him. But we are far from being equal to him. We are his creatures, made in his image, but we are very limited in knowledge, in power, and in our orientation to time and space. As Isaiah records, "'For my thoughts are not your thoughts, neither are your ways my ways,' declares the LORD. 'As the heavens are higher than the earth, so are my ways higher than your ways and my thoughts than your thoughts'" (Isa. 55:8–9).

How well do we even understand one another or ourselves? How well do the best scientists understand our universe, our own planet, or even the human mind and body? We only dimly understand many things that impact our lives physically and emotionally. So we should not be surprised that there are aspects of God's nature that we cannot get clearly in focus. We see that the Scriptures simultaneously affirm both the oneness and threeness of God. And we can understand something of what drove the early church to seek to define the Trinity sufficiently to avoid errors in understanding. But we still find ourselves between understanding and infinite mystery.

Limited Help from Symbols, Patterns, and Analogies

The church has found some things that help a bit with the mystery. Symbols of the Trinity include the triangle and three interwoven rings. These have been used in religious art, including stained glass windows in churches and cathedrals.

We also can find some patterns of three-in-oneness if we look around us in nature. The egg is made up of three parts: yolk, white, and shell. Water can be found as liquid, solid, and gas. The sun in our sky is inseparable from the light it emits and the warmth it brings wherever its light reaches.

Additionally, theologians have used various analogies to ease our intellectual struggle. One is the social analogy. Three human beings can share a common life so closely that they can only be considered as a unit. This is especially evident in a family consisting of a father, mother, and child.

Another is the psychological analogy that attempts to find a faint reflection of three-in-oneness in a human being. One suggestion has been the interaction of mind, emotions, and the will. Somewhat parallel is the suggestion of memory, intelligence, and the will. Paul referred to the "whole spirit, soul and body" (1 Thess. 5:23).

Of course, none of these really unlocks the mystery of God. They can only suggest how three-in-oneness is a viable state of being. They do not explain how God's three-in-oneness operates. As some have put it, it is not that what the Scriptures reveal about God is contrary to reason, but it is above reason—beyond the reach of necessarily limited human reason.

Meaning of Person

One term in the creeds, but not in the Scriptures, is *three persons*. The word *persons* can both help and hinder understanding in our present day. The word *person* is from the Latin *persona*. It meant a "mask (especially one worn by an actor), an actor, a role, a character, a person." Today, a person is a totally distinct individual, a personality. If we think of three personalities in the Trinity, we lose the oneness and end up with three gods, which is contrary to Scripture. If we take the mask aspect too far, we think of one God wearing a different mask at different times and we lose the distinctiveness of the three that the Scriptures set forth. It is true that the Father, Son, and Holy Spirit each had a role in creation, and each has a role in our redemption and sanctification. The term *person* is still the best that has been found. The church has hallowed its use through the centuries to distinguish Father, Son, and Holy Spirit within the oneness of God. But we must use it carefully.

Relationships within the Trinity

As we have seen, the Scriptures clearly state that the Father is God, the Son is God, and the Holy Spirit is God. The Scriptures assign the same divine attributes, such as eternity, to each (see, for example,

Deut. 33:27; Heb. 1:8; 9:14). Yet the Scriptures seem to differentiate between them in their relationship with each other. The Father has a priority within the Trinity—not a priority of time or status or ability, but a priority of relationship.

The Father is the source of all that exists, whether of matter or spirit. Some Scriptures seem to make the Father the source of the Son and the Holy Spirit, although *source* in this context cannot mean there was a time when the Son and the Holy Spirit did not exist. The Father bears that name in part because of his eternal relation to Christ as the "only begotten Son" (compare the King James Version and the New American Standard Bible translations of John 1:14; 3:16; and Heb. 1:5). This does not mean that the Father is more God than the Son, but that somehow the image of a father as the source of a son is like God the Father as the source of God the Son, without a beginning point to that relationship. And John 15:26 tells us that the Holy Spirit "goes out" or "proceeds" (NASB) from the Father. Somehow the image of one in authority sending a representative on a mission is like God the Father eternally being the source of the Spirit, again without a beginning point in that relationship.

Scripture implies that the Father sent the Son on his mission to be "God with us" and "God in the flesh." His purpose was to reconcile us to the Father. His present position is at the Father's right hand, a place of honor but not the primary seat on the throne. And it is at God's right hand that he is interceding for us before the Father. This position, too, pictures a priority of the Father in relation to the Son.

The Bible sets forth very clearly the full and equal deity of the Holy Spirit. And yet it picks up from John 15:26 that the Spirit "proceeds" from the Father, and it adds "from . . . the Son." Jesus substantiated this and said that the Father and Son are both involved in sending the Spirit (see, for example, John 14:16, 26; 15:26; 16:7). Jesus said that the Spirit would take what belonged to Jesus and make it known to the disciples (John 16:13–15). In Romans 8:9, Paul also referred to the Spirit as both the "Spirit of God" and the "Spirit of Christ."

In formulating the creeds, the councils always maintained the same order when referring to the Trinity: Father, Son, and Holy Spirit. It appears clear from the Scriptures that these are the first, second, and third members of the Trinity, in order, as a result of the Father's relation to the Son, and the relation of the Father and the Son to the Spirit.

Involvement of the Trinity in Human Need

One truth comes through again and again. No single member of the Trinity, in isolation from the others, ever does any of the great works on behalf of human beings. We already noted that all three were involved in the creation of humans. As to our redemption, the Father expresses his goodwill toward us by seeking and receiving penitent sinners. Jesus stooped to become a man, to die, to rise again, to reconcile us with God, and to intercede for us with the Father. The Spirit administers grace and affects our conviction, regeneration, sanctification, and glorification—all the results of the Father's loving outreach and Jesus' sacrifice. The Scriptures specify that sanctification is the work of all three (see, for example, 2 Thess. 2:13; 1 Pet. 1:1–2).

The great benefit of the creeds is that they establish the boundaries. This excludes errors. We cannot say less than the Scriptures say or less than what the church has arrived at in the creeds. To say more is to venture into risky speculation.

Which of the analogies of the Trinity is most helpful for you? Why?

WORSHIP OF THE TRINITY

A proper understanding of the Trinity helps us in our worship. While prayer to the Son or the Holy Spirit is not wrong, only one prayer to the Son appears in the New Testament (Acts 7:59) and none to the Holy Spirit. Jesus taught us that when we pray, we are normally to address "Our Father" (Matt. 6:9; Luke 11:2), and Jesus repeatedly set the example for us. We affirm the power of our relationship with God by emphasizing that it is in the Son's name that we pray (see John 15:16; 16:23). Jesus intercedes for us, and the Holy Spirit helps us pray by also interceding for us (see Rom. 8:26–27, 34).

When we thank, praise, and honor the triune God, it is proper to address the Father and to cite what he, the Son, and the Holy Spirit have done and are doing. The Gloria Patri, one of the great aids to worship, sums it all up eloquently:

Glory be to the Father, and to the Son, and to the Holy Ghost. As it was in the beginning, is now, and ever shall be, world without end. Amen.

We began this chapter by circling references in the key passages to the Father, Son, and Holy Spirit and asked what God is like. Now we ask the question: How does the Bible's identification of these three affect the way you worship?

What about now, after all you have studied? Check each response of worship that you believe is stronger in you as a result of your study.

___ Awe	___ Enlightenment	___ Joy
___ Commitment	___ Expectation	___ Love
___ Confidence	___ Gratitude	___ Mystery

How would you describe the doctrine of the Trinity to a friend?

Building Deeper Faith Series

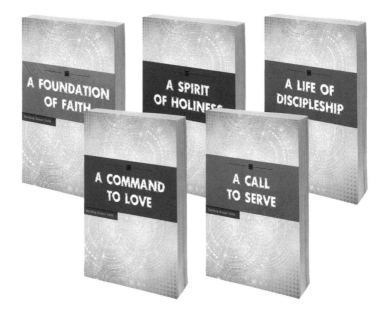

The Building Deeper Faith series offers five solid, biblical, five-week group studies—excellent for strengthening those established in faith and grounding those new to it. Each study's five chapters are relevantly designed to be read and considered by group members during a week, followed up by discussion when the group gathers. These studies are non-sequential and can be studied in any order and are powerful, spiritually foundational tools for deeper discipleship.

A Foundation of Faith
978-0-89827-284-0
978-0-89827-285-7 (e-book)

A Spirit of Holiness
978-0-89827-964-1
978-0-89827-965-8 (e-book)

A Life of Discipleship
978-0-89827-965-5
978-0-89827-967-2 (e-book)

A Command to Love
978-0-89827-968-9
978-0-89827-969-6 (e-book)

A Call to Serve
978-0-89827-970-2
978-0-89827-971-9 (e-book)

1.800.493.7539   wphstore.com